Schott New York

Christopher Cerrone
b.1984

I Will Learn to Love a Person
for Soprano and Piano

text by Tao Lin

Edited by
Scott Wollschleger
Timo Andres

ED 30132

www.schott-music.com

Mainz · London · Madrid · New York · Paris · Prague · Tokyo · Toronto
© 2015 SCHOTT MUSIC CORPORATION, New York · Printed in USA

Contents

Foreword

I've been immersed in Christopher Cerrone's music for several years—performing, discussing, observing the process, and occasionally offering advice—and I've come to think of it all as "vocal music", even in its purely instrumental moments. In his *Invisible Overture*, one of the earliest pieces I heard, an arching woodwind melody emerges from violent string gestures, a premonition of the elegiac opera to follow (*Invisible Cities*). It's a recurring setup in his music: relentless development of a single musical point, until it is almost forced to become a song.

Chris's *I Will Learn to Love a Person* is a piece about relationships—personal, romantic, harmonic, and timbral. Like all of his music, it obsessively controls its limited musical materials in service of big emotional catharses.

There are two contrasting "types" of song in *I Will Learn to Love a Person*. The first, third, and fifth songs emerge from extemporaneous-sounding clouds of harmonies and words: call it text message recitative. The second and fourth songs are bright and motoric, with a candid humor that counteracts the extreme vulnerability of the slow movements. The five songs are masterfully sequenced in a harmonic palindrome, with short interludes of repeated E's acting as pivot points. Harmonic changes are few, and withheld until they feel revelatory.

The relationship of text and music is no less painstaking. It's a rare case in which a musical setting is more than the sum of its parts: Tao Lin's poems, which can be difficult to pin down on the page (are they sincere, or a bit glib?) and the music, so diaphanous at times it seems in danger of evaporating—powerfully concentrate each other in combination. Both elements sound simpler than they actually are. The pianist offhandedly touches some notes, outlining a harmony, over which the singer declaims what could be a series of self-pitying text messages:

> seen from a great enough distance i cannot be seen
> i feel this as an extremely distinct sensation
> of feeling like shit

I Will Learn to Love a Person requires a wide-ranging and nuanced dramatic performance in order to work correctly; perhaps more than a song cycle, it should be thought of as a self-analytical monodrama. Its protagonist is a precocious observer of the world and other people, but also immature and wildly heartbroken; the process of the piece is the discovery that there is, of course, no set of rules that govern human relationships.

Timo Andres
Brooklyn, New York
2015

Preface

In setting out to write my first large vocal piece since completing my opera *Invisible Cities* in 2011, I wanted to work with a different kind of text from Italo Calvino's stylized prose. I hoped to find something more immediate that spoke directly to my life: that of a 29-year-old American, having grown up suburban and with the Internet as a constant presence. It seems at times that "contemporary music" is so intently backwards-looking that it misses what is truly contemporary.

Around this time I read a fantastic essay by the poet Jennifer Moore, "'No discernible emotion and no discernible lack of emotion': On Tao Lin". She discusses Lin's poetry and the "New Sincerity" movement of which he is considered part. New Sincerity poetry is—simply defined—autobiographical, direct, emotional, stripped down, and self-doubting.

What I discovered in Tao Lin's poetry fit perfectly into my compositional style. The thematic links between the poems in his book *Cognitive Behavioral Therapy* allowed me to create a cycle of songs that are similarly connected. The simplicity of the texts also gave me the freedom to try many compositional strategies: sometimes supporting the subject matter with the music, at other times playing against them to highlight certain ambiguities.

In writing these pieces, my hope is to create a work that reflects the strange and beautiful experience of growing up at the turn of the century—and that will continue to have meaning after that moment passes.

Notes on performance:

The voice part should be sung with a minimum of vibrato, reserved perhaps only for particularly expressive moments. Neither a totally vibratoless voice, nor a "bel canto" style feels totally appropriate here.

The pianist should work very hard to blend with the voice, always supporting and never covering.

Christopher Cerrone
Brooklyn, New York
2015

that night with the green sky

it was snowing and you were kind of beautiful
we were in the city and every time i looked up
someone was leaning out a window, staring at me

i could tell you liked me a lot or maybe even loved me
but you kept walking at this strange speed
you kept going in angles and it was confusing me

i think maybe you were thinking that you'd make me disappear
by walking at strange speeds and in a strange and curvy way
but how would that cause me to vanish from earth?

and that hurts
why did you want me gone?
that hurts
why?

why?
i don't know
some things can't be explained, i guess
the sky, for example, was green that night

eleven page poem, page three

my favorite emotions include 'brief calmness
in good weather' and 'i am the only person alive'
without constant reassurance i feel terribly lonely and insane
i have moved beyond meaninglessness, far beyond meaninglessness
to something positive, life-affirming, and potentially best-selling
i have channeled most of my anger into creating and sustaining an
        'angry face'
i have picked up a medium-size glass of coffee
and used it in the conventional way
because I am conventional in all situations, i'll be right back

**I will learn how to love a person and then i will teach
you and then we will know**

seen from a great enough distance i cannot be seen
i feel this as an extremely distinct sensation
of feeling like shit; the effect of small children
is that they use declarative sentences and then look at your face
with an expression that says, 'you will never do enough
for the people you love'; i can feel the universe expanding
and it feels like no one is trying hard enough
the effect of this is an extremely shitty sensation
of being the only person alive; i have been alone for a very long
time
it will take an extreme person to make me feel less alone
the effect of being alone for a very long time
is that I have been thinking very hard and learning about
existence, mortality
loneliness, people, society, and love; i am afraid
that i am not learning fast enough; i can feel the universe
expanding
and it feels like no one has ever tried hard enough; when i cried in
your room
it was the effect of an extremely distinct sensation that 'I am the
only person
alive,' 'i have not learned enough,' and 'i can feel the universe
expanding and making things be further apart
and it feels like a declarative sentence
whose message is that we must try harder'

when i leave this place

the distances i have described in my poems
will expand to find me
but they will never find me

when my head touches your head
your face hits my face at the speed of light

holding it a little

i want to cross an enormous distance with you
to learn the wisdom of lonely animals with low IQs
i want to remember you as a river
with a flower on it

i'll be right back

are you okay?

i don't think telling someone 'don't feel sad' will console them

you need to do whatever you can to make them feel better

whenever your actions make them feel sad

and not stop until they feel better

read my text message and think about it

you just never seem happy with me anymore

even if i make you laugh

i think the damage i've done has become irreversible

i'm surrounded by endless shit

i can't move

where are you

i just had a dream where i came to nyc but i didn't tell you and i took
   the subway

to your apartment and waited for your roommate to come out so i
   could sneak in

then i went into your room and crawled under your sheets from the
   end of your bed

and crawled to your face and kissed you then pet and hugged you

and we fell asleep

happy birthday

i drew you an ugly fish comic
will you visit me today?

i want to hold you

and kiss your face

i miss walking with you at night

World premiere of the chamber version:
August 18, 2013
The Color Field Ensemble
(Amanda DeBoer, Karl Larson, James Fusik, and Owen Weaver)
Chicago, IL

Premiere of the piano and voice version:
April 28th, 2014
Justine Aronson, soprano and Richard Valitutto, piano
Neighborhood Unitarian Universalist Church
Pasadena, CA

This commission has been made possible by the
Chamber Music America Classical Commissioning Program, with generous funding provided by
The Andrew W. Mellon Foundation, and
the Chamber Music America Endowment Fund.

"That Night with the Green Sky" was originally commissioned in a voice and piano version
by OPERA America.

I Will Learn to Love a Person
is for Amanda DeBoer, Karl Larson, James Fusik, and Owen Weaver

I WILL LEARN TO LOVE A PERSON
I. THAT NIGHT WITH THE GREEN SKY

Tao Lin

Christopher Cerrone
(2013)

*) Grace notes on the beat. Quick but not too fast.
**) This last note must be so quiet that it doesn't even register to the audience as an attacked note, just a very quiet resonance.

*attaca in time
do not lift ped.*

II. ELEVEN PAGE POEM PAGE THREE

Tao Lin

Christopher Cerrone

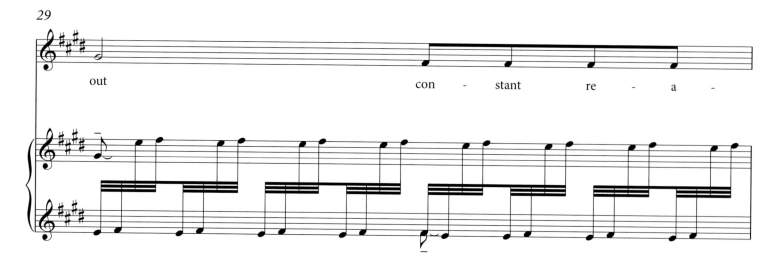

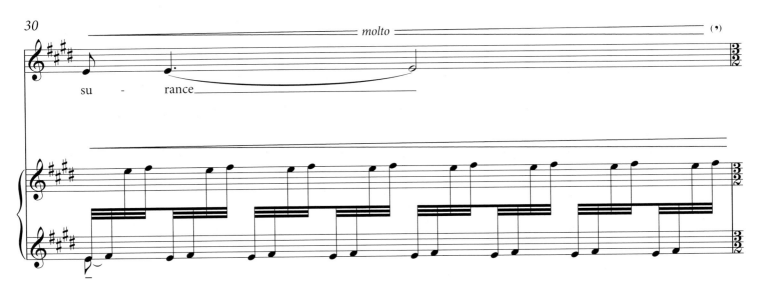

su - rance

p sub, sotto voce, cantabile

I feel ter - ri - bly lone - ly and in -

f

mp

mf

sane

I have moved be-yond mea-ning-less-ness

far be-yond mea-ning-less-ness to some-thing

po-si-tive, life-af-fir-ming and po-ten-tia-ly____ best

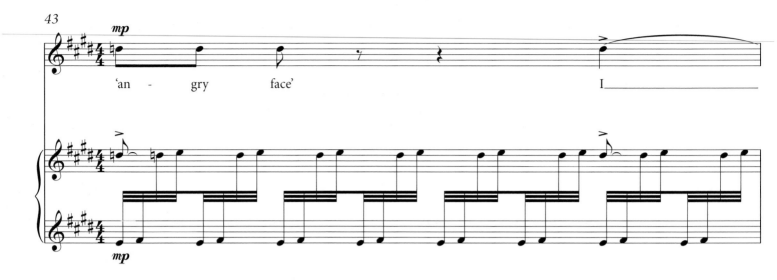

used it in a con -

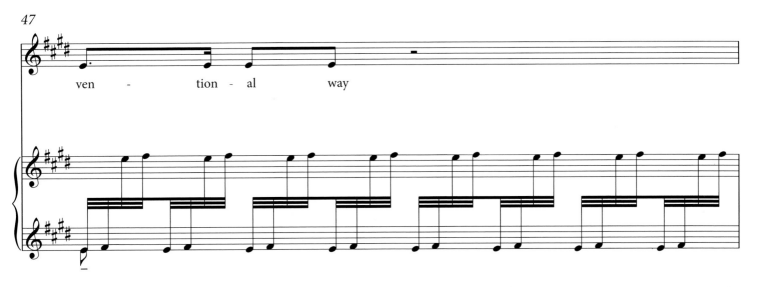

ven - tion - al way

be - - - - -

INTERLUDE

attaca in time
do not lift ped.

III. I WILL LEARN TO LOVE A PERSON AND THEN I WILL TEACH YOU AND THEN WE WILL KNOW

Tao Lin

Christopher Cerrone

Slow, spacious, flowing, fluid ♪ = ca. 106-112

pp sotto voce, childlike, turned inward

seen from a great e-nough dis-tance___ I can-not be seen

(always differentiate the upper and lower voices)

una corda

Ped. ———→ (held from prior song)

4

I feel this as an ex-treme-ly dis-tinct sen-sa-tion of fee-ling like shit The ef-

8

poco accel. *a tempo*

fect of small chil-dren is that they use de-cla-ra-tive sen-ten-ces and look at your face with an ex-

*) Tremolo as quietly and delicately as possible. Almost inaudible. Drop notes from the tremolo when they occur in the upper staff.

I will learn to love a person

*) Omit this note if necessary. Do not roll chord.

IV. WHEN I LEAVE THIS PLACE

Tao Lin

Christopher Cerrone

*) Pronounce "poems" as one syllable.

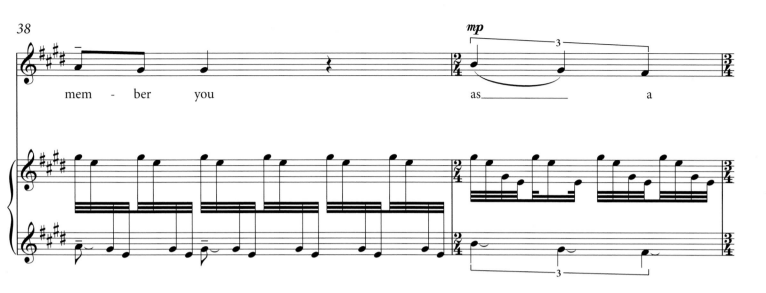

mem - ber you   as_____   a

ri - ver   with   a_____ flo - wer

in it   I'll_____

INTERLUDE

attaca in time
do not lift ped.

V. ARE YOU OK?

Tao Lin

Christopher Cerrone

ED 30132

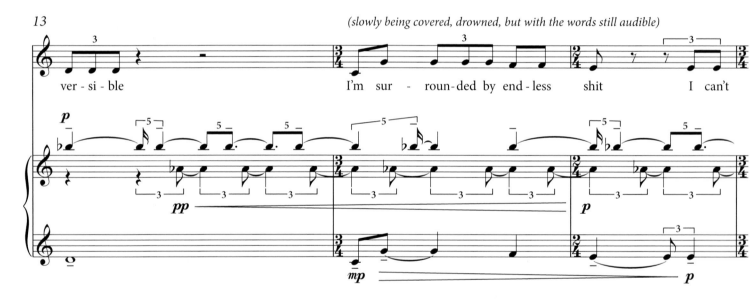

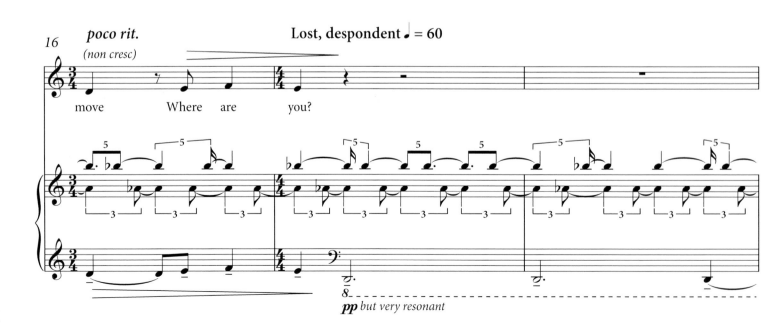

poco a poco rit. until ♩ = ♩.   A strange waltz. ♪ = 138; ♩. = 46

I just had a dream where I came to New York— but I did - n't

slowly lift una corda ————————→ tre corde

tell you I took the sub - way——— to your ap - art - ment and

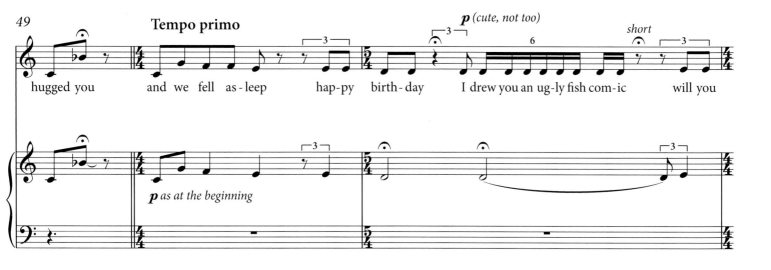

hugged you   and we fell as-leep   hap-py birth-day   I drew you an ug-ly fish com-ic   will you

p as at the beginning

vi-sit me to-day   I want to hold you   and   kiss your cheek   I miss wal-king with you   at

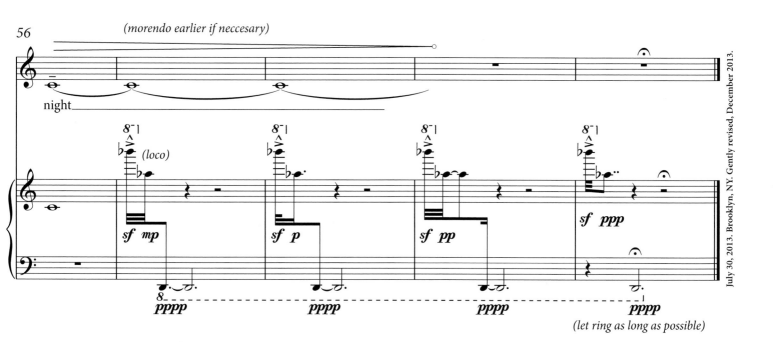

(morendo earlier if neccesary)

night

(let ring as long as possible)

July 30, 2013. Brooklyn, NY. Gently revised, December 2013.